BIBLE VISUALS international

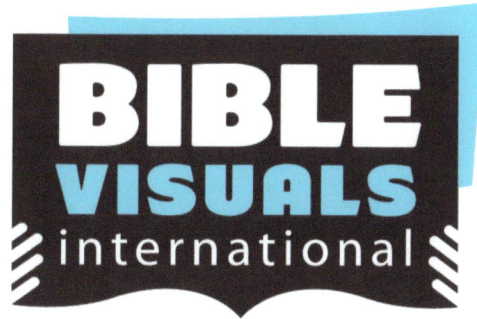

Helping Children See Jesus

ISBN: 978-1-64104-100-3

Salvador of Spain

Authors: Mary Lou Brownell, Katherine Hershey,
Roy Jones, Debby Saint, Karen Weitzel
Illustrator: Debby Saint
Page Layout: Morgan Melton, Patricia Pope

© 2020 Bible Visuals International
PO Box 153, Akron, PA 17501-0153
Phone: (717) 859-1131
www.biblevisuals.org

RELATED ITEMS

To access related items (such as activities, memory verse posters and translated texts) please visit our web store at shop.biblevisuals.org and enter 5510 in the search box on the page.

FREE TEXT DOWNLOAD

To access a FREE printable copy of the teaching text (PDF format) in English or other available languages, enter S5510DL in the search box. Add the item to your cart, and use coupon code XTACSV17 at checkout. Once your order is processed you will receive an email with a link to the free download.

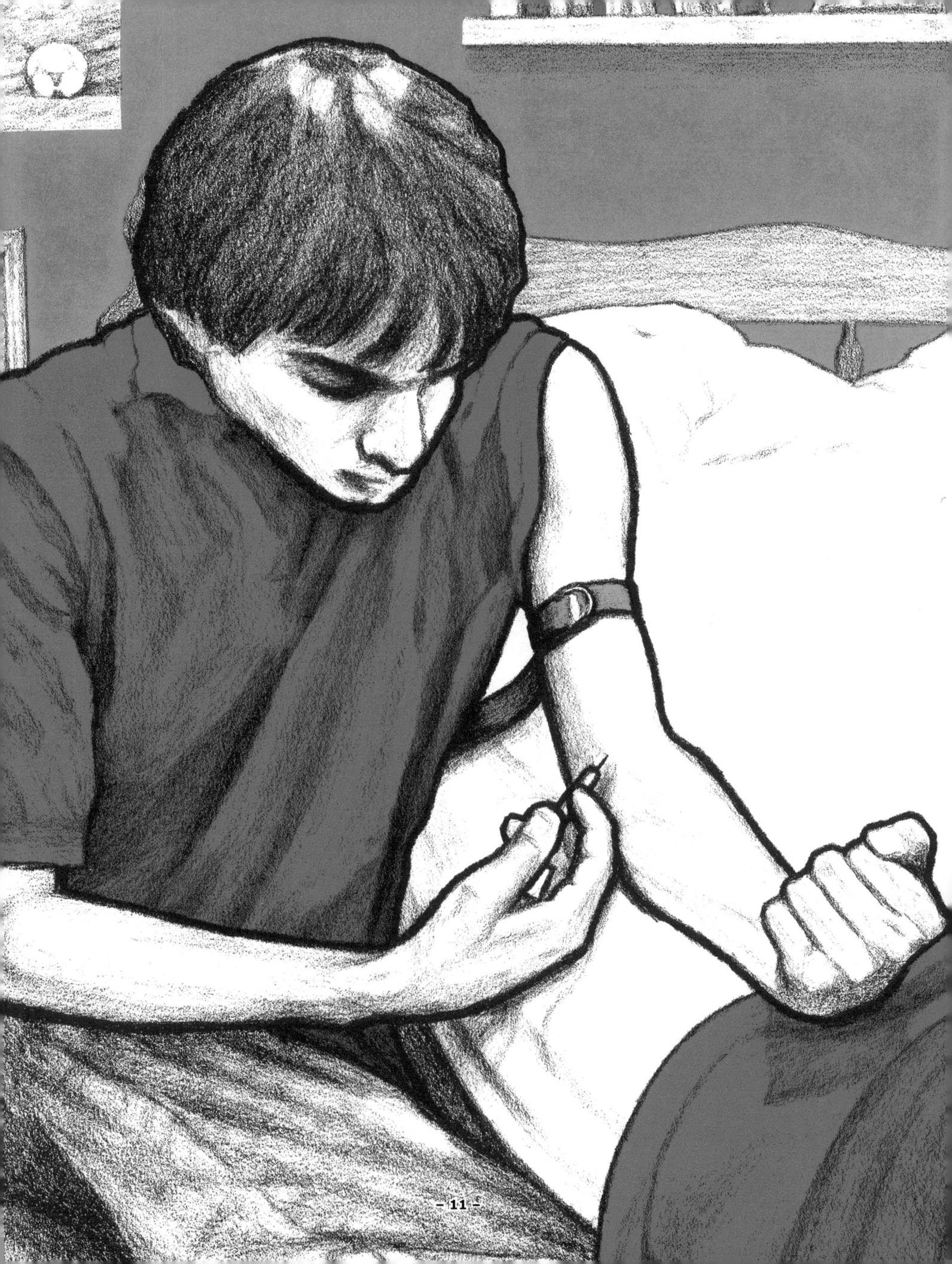

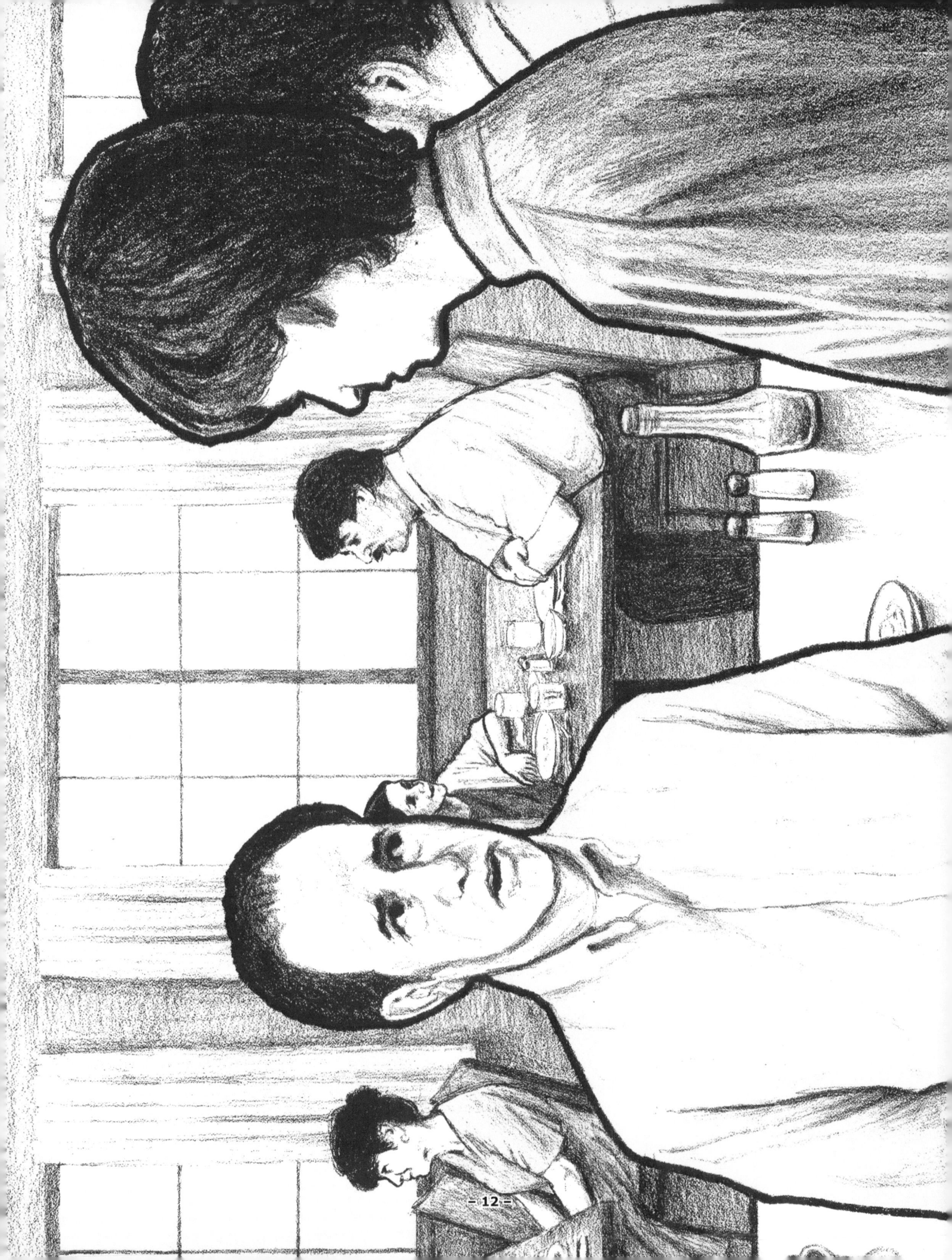

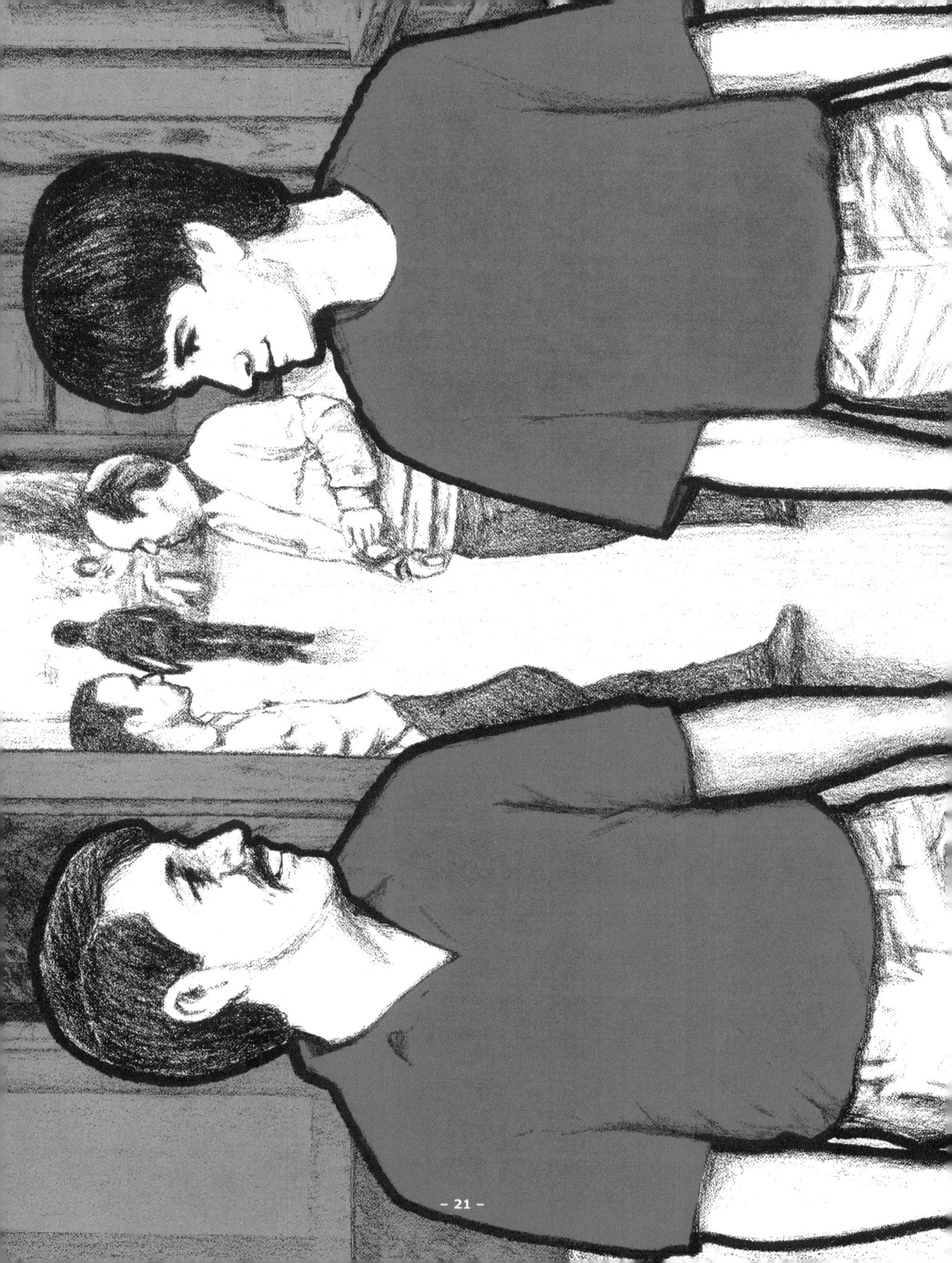

And ye shall know The Truth, and The Truth shall make you free. John 8:32

– 25 –

Of all the neighborhoods in Madrid, the capital of Spain, San Blas was one of the roughest. Anyone who wanted to find drugs or get into trouble could be sure to do so in San Blas.

Show Illustration #1

It was 9:30 in the morning in San Blas. A thin, black-haired boy ambled past the row homes that lined the busy streets. He ducked between women heading to market and children hurrying to school. When he reached the corner he looked both ways as if to make sure no one was watching. Then he dashed across the street and down an alley. Ahead was a large, abandoned factory building with broken windows and a door that hadn't been painted for years. He grabbed the doorknob and pushed the door open. It was cool and dark inside.

Show Illustration #2

"Hey, Salva, you made it!" Salva waited till his eyes adjusted to the darkness and he could see Victor, a friend from school. "It wasn't so hard getting here, was it?"

Salva shook his head. "I just left for school like I always do and when I got close, I went down a different street. Nobody even noticed."

"Well, you'll have a great time today! Firecrackers sound awesome in here!"

Salva grinned. Yes, setting off firecrackers would sound great in here! For a moment Salva thought of his schoolroom and the 100 kids in his class. Would the teacher notice he was absent? He usually tried hard to please his teacher and didn't want to think what would happen if the teacher called on him and he wasn't there to answer. Well, he wouldn't have his hand slapped or his hair pulled by the teacher today!

But what if his mother found out? She would only scream at him as she seemed to do all the time now that there were so many children in their tiny row home. Although Salvador really wanted to please his mother, today he just didn't care! At ten years old he had just skipped school for the first time. Today was going to be a good day.

Show Illustration #3

Salva used to care about things when he was little. He could remember waiting for his dad to come home late at night. Jesus (Hay-SOOS) Miguez worked long hours in a factory an hour away. Sometimes Salva never saw him for several days. But some evenings Salva waited outside their front door with soccer ball in hand, eyes fixed firmly on the end of the street. What fun it was to race to meet Dad, then walk beside him the rest of the way home, matching his own small steps to fit his dad's big ones. Then they would play soccer in the street. Sometimes Salva's two older brothers played against him and his dad; sometimes all three boys played against Dad. What fun they had!

Salva couldn't remember when things had started to change. Because of working longer and longer hours, his dad had begun coming home later and later. "Salva, I'm sorry I can't play soccer with you tonight. I'm just too tired," his dad said many times now.

Salva's disappointment was great, but he knew that without his dad working so long, there just wouldn't be enough money to feed seven children. With Dad away so much, his mother had to take care of him, his five brothers and one sister. Sometimes they fought and his mother would scream to make herself heard and to stop the fighting. She always seemed tired.

Show Illustration #4

Salva knew he and his brothers were partly to blame. They did fight a lot. He could remember the day his older brother Jose wouldn't stop hitting him. Salva punched and kicked and yelled between blows, "Jose, you stop or I'll . . ." Salva pursed his lips and splat! Saliva ran down Jose's cheek. "Mo-o–o-m!" Jose had yelled. The next thing Salva knew was a jolt of pain in the back of his head and the crash of splintering glass. "Salva," his mother yelled, shaking the rest of a broken glass in her hand, "Never spit at anyone. And both of you stop fighting! If you would help me with the work, you wouldn't be causing so much trouble."

Salva had looked down at the floor. He knew he shouldn't be fighting. And he should help with the work. But no other boys in his neighborhood worked at home.

All the boys on his street played soccer. They played so often that they were really good–maybe even good enough to be on a professional team one day! Salva dreamed of that. But even the most exciting game of soccer couldn't take away the thoughts he sometimes had at night after everyone was in bed and the house was quiet. The ache of missing the times he used to spend with his dad; the hurt that came from being yelled at, even though he deserved it; and the heavy feeling knowing that some of the things he had done that day were wrong and that he couldn't go back and start the day over again were jumbled together in his mind. Sometimes Salva thought about what the priest had said.

Show Illustration #5

The black-robed priest who taught religion class at school said that you could pay for the things you had done wrong. "God keeps a list," the priest had said. "He knows all the things you have done today and every day. Each week you must come to church, to confession, and tell me the wrong things you have done. I will then tell you what God expects you to do to pay for them." Salva had squirmed in his seat. He looked at Victor beside him and Manuel in front of him. He did not want to talk to anyone, not even his best friends, about saying mean things, about spitting, about lying, about fooling around, about not helping his mother.

Salva had slid down in his seat and folded his arms defiantly across his chest. The memory of the only time he'd gone to confession popped into his mind. The priest had gotten angry with him that day. Salva could still hear his sharp words, "Salvador, pay attention! What's the matter with you?" And then the priest had hit him on the back of his head. Salva unconsciously rubbed his head as if feeling the pain all over again. His parents could go to church, but Salva would never go again.

Show Illustration #2

But Salvador forgot about school and priests and his family the day he skipped school. He had firecrackers, friends, and a whole day to do as he pleased. "Hey, Victor," he called, "will you let me light the next one?"

Salva lit the firecracker and jumped back before it exploded with a tremendous echoing boom. *What a day this is going to be*, he thought. And it was a perfect day because no one, neither his teachers nor his parents, noticed that he had not gone to school. *Wow!* Salva thought. *I'll have to do this again!*

Show Illustration #6

A few days later Salva sat in religion class at school listening to the priest talk about special people who had been outstandingly good when they were alive. "We call these people 'saints,'" he said. "And it could be that if you are extra careful to go to confession, to pay for your sins, to give money to the church, and to pray, one of you will become a saint and have a statue made of you like the ones of St. Matthew and St. Anne in our church." Salva looked sideways at Victor seated beside him, and the corners of his mouth turned up. In his mind he could see a statue of him and Victor perched high above the people's heads in church as they recited "Our Father which art in Heaven. . . ." Salva wanted to snicker, but he pulled his lips together just before the priest stared hard at him.

But the picture of him and Victor stayed. Salva looked down at his thin arms, his red shirt, his black pants, his raggedy sneakers. In his mind they were turning into smooth white marble. *What would it feel like to be made out of marble? Cold and stiff, never able to change position.*

Thump! Salva did not see the hand swinging toward the back of his head, but he did feel the pain. "Salvador, pay attention!" the priest scolded angrily.

Salva's face grew red. Everyone in the class stared at him. Salva scowled at the priest who stalked toward the front of the room. He might have expected his mother, or another one of his teachers, to hit him on the back of the head. The priest was supposed to be closer to God than anyone else. And this was the second time he had been struck by a priest! Salva fixed his eyes on the priest's face, but inside he was not listening. *If that's how God is going to treat me*, he thought, *then I don 't need Him.*

The next three years Salva went to school less and less although he always left home as if he were going to school and returned at the right time in the afternoon. Salva and his friends formed a gang. One day one of the boys brought cigarettes he had stolen from his parents. Some of the boys snatched the cigarettes and lit them quickly. Salva watched the smoke curl toward the ceiling of the abandoned factory before he lit his first cigarette. Salva's first puff almost choked him. The taste was bitter and the smoke burned his throat. But to prove he was "tough" he kept puffing on the cigarette. The next day smoking was a little easier, and in a week Salvador was smoking without even thinking what he was doing. Once or twice he thought of

his parents and how upset they would be if they found out about his smoking and how they stole cigarettes from parked cars. *Salvador, we don't want you to smoke cigarettes like the other boys in the neighborhood. Smoking will harm your lungs.* But Salva's parents were too busy to notice. *Besides,* Salva thought, *my friends accept me when I smoke, so what else matters?*

When Salva was 13 he dropped out of school. "Most of my friends have stopped going to school," Salvador defended himself to his parents. "I've already gone through eight grades. That's enough school for me!"

Show Illustration #7

One day not too long after Salva dropped out of school he returned from spending the day with the gang. He shoved open the door. Someone was clanking pans and crackling paper. Salva, curious, walked to the kitchen. "Mom, what are you doing?" he cried in alarm. He watched her pack the pans in a box, then looked around the room. The cupboard was empty. "Where are our dishes?"

"They're packed, Salva. We're moving. Your father found a bigger apartment in Coslada. It's only ten miles away."

"Moving!" Salva screamed. "We can't move. All my friends are here!"

"We are moving, son," his father said firmly as he entered the kitchen with an empty box. "Your older brothers will stay here in this home because they have jobs here in San Blas, but you and the other children are moving to Coslada."

"Please, Dad, let me stay in San Blas," Salva begged.

"I'm sorry, Salvador, but you have to come with us. You'll make new friends in Coslada," his father assured him.

I'll never have friends like I have here in San Blas, Salva thought bitterly. But to his surprise, he found a new group of guys who, like him, had decided that being on the street was better than sitting in school. Moving to Coslada was not so bad after all!

But Salva's hours of roaming the streets ended quickly. "Salva, I have something to tell you," his father announced one evening. "I've found a job for you in that restaurant down the street. The hours are long. You start at nine o'clock in the morning and may have to stay till midnight, but you will be learning a trade and earning some money. Your mother and I think it will be good for you and will keep you out of trouble."

Show Illustration #8

Early the next morning, Salva was at the restaurant listening to his new boss. "Salva, you will serve drinks at the bar. There are lots of different kinds, so Miguel here will help you learn. And remember, we want to keep our customers happy."

Salva grinned. He was good at cracking jokes and making people laugh. Maybe he was going to like this job.

The men urged Salva to try the liquor he served to them. "Salva, this drink is my favorite," one of the older men at the bar would say, sipping from the mug Salva had just handed him. "Why don't you mix one for yourself?" Another would say, "No, mine is better. Try this one, Salva."

Soon Salva knew the taste of different drinks. At times he drank so much that he couldn't think or talk clearly. "You're getting drunk, Salva, just like the rest of us," the men called and then laughed at Salva's unsteady walk. Salva laughed with them. Getting drunk was a new kind of fun; his troubles didn't seem important. In fact, nothing seemed important except having a good time. He rather liked getting drunk until he woke up the next morning with a terrible throbbing in his head.

Salva didn't like that, but he did like stealing money from the cash register and cigarettes from behind the counter. Free liquor, extra money, free cigarettes. *This job isn't so bad after all!* he thought.

Show Illustration #9

Salva visited his two older brothers in San Blas whenever he could. One day Jose and Javi were smoking cigarettes that looked different. "What are you smoking, Jose?" asked Salva.

"You haven't tried this yet? Here, it's marijuana. Makes you feel great! You can see, feel, and hear everything in a totally new way. Marijuana makes you forget about anything that's bothering you."

"Sounds good to me," said Salva. He took the cigarette Jose handed him and began to puff. Soon he began to feel very calm, happy, almost silly. "I like this," he said to Jose. "I could smoke marijuana all day."

"It costs money," Jose replied, "but you have plenty of that. Help yourself."

So Salva smoked and the marijuana made him forget all the yelling and fighting at home. As he puffed, his memories of lying about skipping school and stealing from the restaurant faded away; plus all the other memories of disobeying his parents and his teachers; and all the other times of treating people meanly. Something the priest said so long ago flickered in his mind. "A person must pay for his sins." Salva felt as if a huge weight was pressing down on his shoulders. There was no way that he, Salvador, could pay for his sins. Not with a list of sins stretching as far back as he could remember. And then that wonderful feeling from the marijuana overcame him and his sins were no longer important.

On later visits, Jose and Javi gave Salvador different kinds of pills and powders. "They make you forget your troubles even more than marijuana did, Salva." They urged him to take them. "The only problem, Salva, is that the high lasts only for a while. You have to keep taking drugs, Salva, to keep that high feeling. And the drugs cost money."

Salva began selling drugs not only to his friends, but also to his brothers. But still he needed more money. "How do you get your money?" he asked his brothers one day.

Show Illustration #10

"Come with us tonight, and we'll show you," they told him. Jose, Javi and Salva waited until late evening when the street was still. Quietly they left the apartment and walked stealthily down the street. Jose leaned over and whispered to Salva. "We want to find a car that's in the shadows or out of sight. When we find one Javi will be the lookout for us and stand far enough away so that he can watch the entire street to see if anyone's coming. Then you and I will get to work."

It didn't take long to find a car. Salva crouched in the shadows as Jose, making almost no sound, worked to remove the hubcaps. Moving quietly to the front of the car he carefully unscrewed the headlights and passed them to Salva who laid them on the ground. One of the headlights fell over and rolled on the gravel. The boys froze. Jose quickly took a wire from his pocket and wiggled it in the door until it unlocked. "Open the door, Salva," he whispered. "We want the cassette player."

The job was finished in less than ten minutes. Jose glanced at Salva and smiled. "We got ourselves some more drug money when we sell these headlights, hubcaps and cassette player. Nothing to it."

"That was great!" Salva whispered. He didn't want to think how the person who owned the car would feel the next morning. All that really mattered was that they had more money to buy drugs.

Show Illustration #11

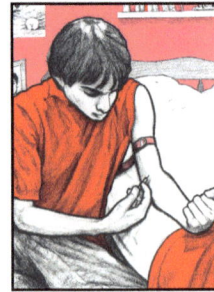

By now Salva was using a different kind of drug, a drug he injected with a needle. Heroin gave him a warm, pleasant feeling at first, then a sleepiness that made him feel as if he could hardly hold his head up. He felt as if he had no troubles at all. But when the sleepy time ended, Salva had to shoot more heroin within 12 hours or he would begin shaking, and have chills, sweating, fever, runny eyes and nose, vomiting, diarrhea, twitching and hurting muscles. (*Teacher:* Use discretion in what symptoms you tell.) Salva had to keep taking heroin or he would be sick. He was "hooked" or "addicted" to the drug at age 16 and he did not know anyone who had gotten off drugs once he was hooked.

Salva continued to work and to steal and to take drugs. One night he discovered that the police had raided his brothers, apartment and arrested everyone they found there. Javi and Jose both spent time in jail. *I won't get caught,* Salva told himself. *I'm too smart to go to jail.*

Salva was eighteen now and seldom went home. He rarely saw his father, but on one visit home his father suggested, "Salva, I think it's time that you joined the army."

"The army!" Salva exploded. "I don't want to join the army!"

"You're 18 now. All Spanish men are required to spend time in the army. You won't be able to get a decent job until you do."

Salva thought about his father's suggestion for days and days. His father was right.

On the army base outside of Madrid, Salva continued taking and selling drugs. He liked what drugs did for him and he liked the power that selling drugs gave him. "You can always depend on Salva getting the stuff," his buddies said as he took their money. In time, though, he was caught and sent to jail for three months. But even that didn't stop him from taking and selling drugs when he was released from jail.

When Salva got out of the army, his father decided to help him and Jose start a restaurant. Salva had experience in a bar and Jose was a cook. "I'm willing to put up some money to help you get started," their dad promised. So Salva and Jose opened their restaurant and they did well, except for one problem–drugs. Both brothers needed more money than they were being paid for working, so they started doing what they already had lots of experience doing–stealing. They stole from the cash register while at work and, late at night after the restaurant closed, from cars on the street. They were almost caught several times. "We gotta be more careful," they told each other.

Show Illustration #12

Months went by. Salva's father began to wonder why the restaurant didn't seem to be making any money. Finally he had to ask them. Early one morning he walked into the restaurant. "Jose, Salva, what's going on here? Why don't you seem to be making any profit?"

Jose looked at Salva. Salva looked at Jose. Then Jose's face grew very serious. "Dad, we've been spending the money on drugs."

"Drugs! Not drugs!" Their father's face was pale.

Salva spoke quickly. "Jose may think he has a problem with drugs, but I don't. I'm just fine."

Their father shook his head as if he couldn't believe what he was hearing. "Drugs! My two boys on drugs!" Tears rolled down his cheeks.

Jose and Salva looked at each other. They felt awful to see their strong father crying.

"Dad, it's not your fault. Other people have kids on drugs. We'll get out of it somehow."

But their father still looked as if his whole world had fallen apart. "Jose, Salva, I will help you. I will do whatever I can to help you be free of drugs. Oh, my boys! If only I had known sooner!"

A few days later their father told them that he had made a doctor's appointment for them.

Sitting outside the doctor's office with their father, Jose and Salva tried to look at magazines. Finally it was their turn.

"What can I do for you?" asked the doctor as the three of them walked into his office.

"Well," Salva's father said, clearing his throat, "my two sons seem to have picked up a drug habit. They're both addicted to heroin."

"Heroin?" The doctor's eyebrows raised sharply. "Drug addicts?" He paused for a moment, then spoke nervously. "I'm afraid I can't see them. There's nothing I can do to help them."

"You can't see them? You're a doctor. Surely you can help them," their father pleaded. "You can do something for them, can't you?"

The doctor stood up. He would not look at Jose and Salva, only at their father. "As I said before, I can't see them. There is no help for a person addicted to drugs."

Chapter 2

Outside the office Salva looked at Jose with fear and anger in his eyes. "So the doctor thinks there's no hope for us. We might as well not bother trying to stop doing drugs." Salva said nothing more as they walked home, but frightening and confusing thoughts chased through his mind. *I'll never get off drugs now. If there's no hope, why should I care? But I'm tired of doing drugs. But am I that tired? Drugs make me feel so good–for a while.*

Although Salva didn't spend much time at home, he began to notice a change in his mother. She had started going to meetings in a missionary's home where they read and talked about a book called the Bible.

What's so special about the Bible? Salva scoffed. He remembered seeing the priest hold a black book in his hand and tell stories from it in religion class. But the priest never told the students to read it.

Show Illustration #13

"Salva, the Bible is different from all other books," his mother explained. "The Bible is God speaking directly to us. He used people to write down the words, but the words are directly from Him."

How can God speak directly? Salva thought as he left the house to buy drugs. *That's crazy.* Whenever Salva thought about God–and he tried not to, but sometimes the thought came anyway–he saw a huge judge with an angry face just waiting for Salva to reach the end of his life so He could give Salva all the punishment he deserved. And maybe a bit more. God speaking directly? Salva did not want to hear it.

But his mother kept attending the meetings and a church started by the same missionaries. One day she returned excited and happy.

"What happened to make you so happy?" Salva asked in amazement.

"I finally understand what Jesus did when He died on the cross," she said. "I used to think that He paid for only part of my sins. I had to pay for all the rest. I thought that God was angry with me because, no matter how hard I tried, I could never do enough good things, say enough prayers, give enough money, or go to confession often enough to pay for the sins Jesus didn't pay for."

"Then I began studying the Bible. And that made me feel even worse. It said that even the best things I do, when compared to how good God is, are only like filthy rags."

"Filthy rags? That's ugly!" Salva exclaimed.

His mother ignored his outburst. "But then I saw what Jesus did with all those filthy rags. He took them all, all of my sins, on Himself when He hung on the cross. It was as if He had done the sins. But He had never done one sin in His life."

She spoke softly. "When the nails were pounded into His hands, it was because of my sin. He was being punished for me, for my sins–all of them."

There were tears in her eyes, but joy in her voice. "Today I told Jesus that I believed He died for my sins and that I trusted Him instead of myself to pay for them. I asked Him to forgive me for all of my sins. And He has. That awful weight of trying to do something that was impossible is gone. I'm forgiven."

Forgiven! Salva's eyebrows raised and he looked at his mother quizzically. *Could it be that I could be forgiven too?* For a brief instant Salva began to believe that maybe that could happen for him. *But no*, he thought, despair overcoming him. *I'm a heroin addict. Even if Jesus had somehow done something about my sins, He could never set me free from heroin. Heroin is stronger than anything. I might as well forget what Mom has said.*

But because Salva lived in the same house, when he was home, he couldn't help seeing how different she acted. She still screamed at times, but when she talked to Jesus about it, she believed that she was forgiven. "Jesus paid for all my sins," she said, "even the ones I'm going to do tomorrow, and the next day, and the next."

Salva only shook his head. *This doesn't make any sense to me.*

"Salva," his parents said one evening, "there's a place in Madrid that helps drug addicts be free of drugs. It's Christian. Would you be willing to go?"

Salva hesitated. He wanted to stop taking drugs. It was getting harder to get money to continue buying drugs.

"Jose is going," his mother added. Her face looked as if she were wishing very hard. "It would be wonderful if both of you could be free of drugs."

"All right, Mom. I'll go," Salva said grudgingly.

At the center the doctor questioned both boys. "Do you want to be free of drugs?"

Jose looked soberly at the doctor. "I really want to stop, but I can't."

"And what about you, Salva?" the doctor asked.

Salva laughed rudely, then boasted. "If I had the money, I'd never quit taking drugs!"

"We can't let you stay," the doctor told him. "You have to want to stop taking drugs. Jose may enter the program though."

Show Illustration #11

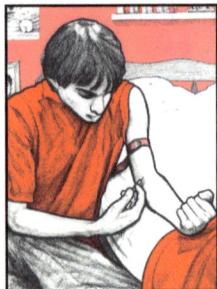

Days, weeks, months went by as Salva continued stealing, selling and using drugs, feeling blissfully peaceful and then having sharp, awful cravings for more drugs. Salva felt as if he was on a horrible ride down a steep hill and couldn't get off. He went to his dad. "Could you talk to the missionary and find out if there's another place I could try to get off drugs?"

The missionary knew of another drug rehabilitation center, but it was six hours north of Madrid. Salva watched the scenery change from a busy city to mile after mile of country with few towns or houses. *Where on earth are we going?* he thought in alarm. *What am I getting myself into?*

Salva got out of the car and looked around. *This place doesn't even have electricity. And everyone is carrying Bibles!* At the end of the first day Salva had only one thought in mind. *I gotta plan how to get out of here*, he said to himself. *These people are crazy talking about God and the Bible so much. What good can God do for me?*

But everyone at the center was friendly and included Salva in all the activities. *Maybe God can help me*, Salva thought again. *I'll try to stick it out.*

But four days later Salva and two others stood at the roadside hitchhiking their way back to Coslada. *I had to leave*, Salva told himself, his hands and legs shaking. *No heroin for three days. I feel as if I'm crawling out of my skin.*

Back home in Coslada, Salva bought heroin and injected it into his arm. What relief!

Show Illustration #14

"Hey, Salva, how did it go?"

Salva opened his bleary eyes and saw Jose. There was something different about his face. He was smiling. His eyes were bright and alert.

"It was okay," Salva replied passively. "The people were cool. Kinda weird about God, but other than that, pretty nice. No heroin though. I had to leave early." He paused. "What's with you, Jose? You look happy."

"Salva, I know this Jesus stuff sounds weird to you, but it's Jesus who's given me this happiness that I have now. I was so out of control, a slave to drugs, wrecking my body, treating other people's property as if it were my own just because I had to have money for drugs. But at the center, they kept telling me from the Bible that God already knew how rotten I was. He sent Jesus to be punished for every single one of my sins. They told me that if I would ask Jesus, He would forgive me and make me like a new person. Salva, I did that."

The room was still. Then Salva spoke wistfully. "Well, I'm glad it worked for you, Jose. Really glad. But I don't think it would for me."

"But it will, Salva; it will!"

Show Illustration #15

Salva saw how different Jose acted. He was happy and Salva wanted that same happiness. *Maybe if I read the Bible I can find what Jose found*, Salva thought. He picked up the Bible his mother had placed beside his bed and read it when no one was looking. *God, why is there so much evil in the world? Why do You seem so far away?*

Sometimes at night, alone in his room, Salva would cry. "God, if You are real, please show Yourself to me. I wish I could find what Jose and Mother have, but it just doesn't seem to be there for me."

One day his mother stopped him on his way to his room. "Salva, would you like to come to camp with your father and me? It's at a beautiful place out in the country."

Camp? Salva thought as he Looked down at his mother. *Maybe being there would help me stay away from drugs.* "Yeah, I'll go," he said gruffly, not wanting her to know how much he really wanted to attend.

The camp was beautiful and the people fun to be with. They were happy just like his mother and Jose. Seeing their happiness made Salva feel left out. He was so different from them too. For the first time Salva felt uneasy about his uncombed hair. No other men walked around with their shirts unbuttoned.

Show Illustration #16

Salva noticed a pretty, young woman with dark hair who always seemed ready to talk to him. He didn't know she was a missionary who had heard his mother praying for him! The second day he invited her to go canoeing.

As they paddled down to the end of the lake, Ellie asked, "Salva, are you a happy man?"

"No," he replied, his face serious and very sad. "I'm miserable."

Ellie looked at him. "I am a happy person, Salva. Will you let me tell you how you can become a joyful person too?"

"Yes," Salva answered slowly. But he didn't ask her to tell him then. He was quiet and Ellie couldn't read his thoughts. *Maybe this happiness isn't for everyone. Maybe for everyone but me. I don't see how a heroin addict can be happy.*

Show Illustration #17

After canoeing Salva saw John, one of the missionaries, sitting by himself reading. "Hey," Salva asked, walking up to him, "what are you reading? Must be pretty good to keep you from all the others. Sounds like they're all having a good time."

John held up the book. "It was written years ago by a man named Charles Spurgeon. He wanted to explain salvation. It's called *All of Grace*."

"Can I read it?"

John laughed. "It's all marked up from me trying to learn new Spanish words. I'll get another one for you when we get back to Madrid."

"I'd like to read it now, even if it's marked up," Salva replied.

"You really do? Well, okay," John said handing the book to Salva. "Just don't say I didn't warn you about my scribbling."

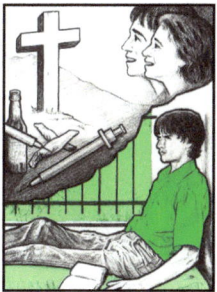

Show Illustration #18

Salva carried the book to a quiet spot and opened it. Minutes passed, then half an hour. As Salva read, a hard place inside him softened, a place that had said there was no hope. It was as if a tiny seed of hope had been planted. The book said some of the same things his mother, the missionaries and Jose had told him from the Bible. Salva began to understand what he read. Hope grew stronger in his heart.

Then a thought like a giant foot stamped and smashed his hope. *Heroin! Maybe Jesus could forgive me, but can He set me free from heroin? No one,* Salva said to himself, *not even Jesus can set me free from heroin!*

Salva was miserable. Part of him wanted so much to hope–and believe–while another part of him said so convincingly, "There's no hope."

The next day was the last day of camp. Each person packed his belongings to be ready to leave right after lunch. Salva's heart was heavy. Camp was almost over and he had not found the happiness everyone else seemed to have.

As Salva finished the last of his dessert, the camp director stood up and announced, "We have a surprise for you. You have two more hours to stay and swim." Across the room Salva saw Ellie. He remembered she'd said, "If you ever want me to tell you why I have joy inside of me, please ask." Salva stood up and walked toward her. "Would you want to walk by the woods?"

Show Illustration #19

"Yes," Ellie replied, and they left the dining area. They stopped under a large tree and sat down. Salva looked at Ellie and asked, "Can I tell you what it has been like for me to be addicted to drugs?"

"Yes, Salva. I'd be glad to listen," Ellie answered quietly.

So Salva began, way back with his first puff on a cigarette and continued all the way to his addiction to heroin. "No one can help me, Ellie," Salva said. "Not even Jesus."

"Salva, you do not know Jesus. If you knew Him, you would not be afraid to trust Him to free you from heroin. Nothing, absolutely nothing, is too hard for Him. If you ask Him, He will deliver you."

"No, Ellie. Three weeks ago my parents paid for me to go to a drug rehabilitation center. Do you know what I did the very last day?" Salva looked away from Ellie. "I took some more heroin. The very last day." He turned back to the missionary. "I couldn't tell Dad and Mom. I was too ashamed. Don't you see, Ellie. Nobody can help me."

"Salva, Jesus is all-powerful. He created the world. He made everything. Heroin is not stronger than He is."

Salvador took a deep breath. "Suppose I do pray the sinner's prayer now. All these dear people at camp will hug me and cry for joy. And then, after a week or even before that they will be hurt when they learn that I have gone back to heroin. Believe me, Ellie, I know guys who have stayed away from drugs for two years and then gone back to them. There is no way I can be set free from heroin."

"Jesus *is* able, Salva. He can set you free–once and for all. You won't have to fall back on taking heroin again. His power is greater than any other power."

Salva was silent. Then he spoke. "All right, Ellie. I will pray."

Bowing his head, he said, "God, I believe You can forgive my sin. Prove Your power and deliver me. Save me, please! Amen."

Show Illustration #20

When he lifted his head, Ellie asked, "Did you mean it, Salva?"

"Yes, I did."

"Where is Jesus now?"

"In me." Salva smiled. The awful weight inside was gone. Instead there was peace and joy that Ellie had talked about.

"But please, Ellie," Salva said, his face serious again, "don't tell anybody about this. Not yet. I want to see God make a difference in my life before I tell anyone what I did."

Salva rode back to Coslada with Roger, the missionary pastor of the church his mother attended. Salva wanted to tell Roger that he had asked God to save Him. But he did not want to disappoint anyone, so he only said that he had made some decisions at camp.

When Ellie returned home she phoned Roger. "Roger, even though Salva asked me not to tell anyone, I am telling you because you are the pastor of his family. Salva prayed this afternoon and asked God to save him."

"Ellie, that's wonderful!" Roger exclaimed. "I thought he seemed different on the way home. You've given me the best news I've had for a long time. I'll keep quiet and wait for Salva to tell me about his decision."

When Salva woke the next morning he realized he didn't care about heroin at all. There was no pull inside him to shoot the drug and he wasn't even sick. He could hardly believe it. Jesus had delivered him! Instead of wanting heroin, Salva wanted to learn more about Jesus. Instead of thinking about how he could get heroin, he lay in bed and planned how he could spend time with Ellie and Roger.

Three days passed. No desire for heroin. Then four, five and six. Still no desire for heroin. Only a great desire to read the Bible, to pray and to be with other Christians.

Show Illustration #21

Roger watched Salva every time he visited the missionary's family. After a week he could wait no longer. "Salva, are you or are you not going to tell me?"

Salva looked at the pastor with a grin on his face. "Tell you what?"

"Tell me why you're so different. Ever since we returned from camp I've seen a change in you."

"You really think I'm different?"

"Yes, Salva. Something's happened to you."

"Well, Pastor Roger, I–I asked Jesus to save me."

"Salva! That's wonderful!" Roger threw his arms around Salva and hugged him. "I'm so happy! We're all happy for you!"

Salva spent as much time as he could with Ellie and Roger and his family. But it wasn't long before he ran into some of his drug-addict friends.

Show Illustration #22

"Hey, Salva, what's happened? We haven't seen you around for a while. I bet you found a new kind of drug and are keeping it a secret from the rest of us."

"No, guys. This will sound really crazy to you, but I'm off drugs. Jesus has set me free. I'm not taking heroin anymore."

His friends looked shocked, disbelieving. One spoke up, "You're kidding, aren't you, Salva?"

"No, I'm not. It was at camp, more than a week ago. I asked God to save me from my sins and from heroin. And He did. I don't have any desire for heroin any more."

His friends were quiet. Then one of them spoke. "Well, you sure look different."

"I am, but not because of anything I did. I had a hard time believing that God could be stronger than heroin. I thought nothing could be stronger than heroin. But when I asked Him, He proved that He is stronger."

Salva was glad to tell his friends about Jesus. He wanted them to be free the way he was. But at the same time he was afraid to spend too much time with them. One day not too much later he ran into some friends again. He waited for a chance to tell them about Jesus, but before he realized it, he was taking drugs right along with them. The drugs made him sick, very sick. He had to leave right away.

"Jesus, please forgive me," Salva prayed as he walked, half bent over, towards home. "I wasn't thinking. Even though I feel awful, thank you for making me sick. I don't ever want to do drugs again. Maybe I should stay away from my friends until I'm stronger. Then I can go back and tell them about how You can forgive and help them."

So Salva stayed away from his old friends. He spent a lot of time with Roger and his family, arriving early in the morning and staying late at night. He soon became like one of the family. Roger's children grew to love him as their own brother.

Salva approached Roger one day. "Could I be baptized?"

"Why, of course, Salva. You've shown that you believe and want to follow God. There's someone else who wants to be baptized," Roger added.

"Who?" Salva asked.

"Your father, Salva. After seeing the change in your life, your father realized he needed Jesus to save Him. Now that he has believed, he wants to be baptized too."

Months went by. Salva began working part-time at a school for missionaries' children. He still thought much about his old friends and prayed for them. He also asked God to show him when to go back and tell them about Jesus.

Show Illustration #22

One by one, and sometimes by twos or threes, Salva began talking with his old friends. Francisco started going to church with him. Soon he asked God to save him.

Salva was asked to talk to other drug addicts. One of them told Salva, "Nobody can help me." But after talking to Salva he felt differently. "I knew you as a drug addict," he said. "You were much deeper into drugs than I am now. But you are normal now. I believe what you said about Jesus, and I believe God will save me too."

Sometimes Salva met policemen who had known him when he was addicted to heroin. "Salva, I can hardly believe it's you," said one. "You were skin and bones the last time I saw you. I thought for sure you would have died by now."

Salva often saw kids on the streets who behaved as he once had. He knew they could end up being drug addicts just as he had been. So Salva began to spend time with the older boys at church, helping them to know how to follow Jesus. He even began teaching and preaching. And when a drug addict wanted to talk with him, Salva listened. *I remember all the patience and love that were given to me*, he thought. *I want to give the same patience and love to these guys.*

Show Illustration #23

One day Jose walked into Salva's room. "You know that I went to the doctor to see why I have been getting sick lately, don't you? He found out what's wrong with me." Jose swallowed hard and then whispered, "I have AIDS."

"No, Jose!" Salva exclaimed as he threw his arms around Him. "Was the doctor sure?"

"Yes."

Salva felt as if someone had punched him hard in the stomach. *There is no medicine that will cure AIDS*, he thought. *Jose will eventually die.* The inside of him was filled with pain.

"Jose, did the doctor say how you got it?"

"He said it probably came from dirty needles. You know, those ones we picked up off the factory floor. Or maybe the ones we shared with our friends."

"Then I might have AIDS too."

"I hope not, Salva! I would feel awful!"

"Jose, whatever is ahead for us, we know that Jesus is in it with us. Sometimes people live for years after they find out they have AIDS."

"The doctor told me that," said Jose. "Whatever time I have left, it all belongs to Jesus."

Not too much later Salva heard the same news. The doctor's words were hard for him to hear. "Salva, you also have AIDS like your brother."

I don't want to die, Salva thought. *I want to live! For a long, long time. But Lord, whatever time I have, please help me to live for you*, he prayed.

Salva continued to build his own house even though he knew he probably would only live there for a few years. Roger and his family took him to America where he told people what Jesus had done for him. When he returned to Spain he continued to teach and lead in the church in Coslada.

Show Illustration #24

Salva was now 29 years old. For some time he had been growing weaker and thinner. Knowing that his birthday was coming up shortly before Christmas, his friends planned a surprise party. Over 100 attended. Salva was overjoyed to see them.

Salva spent Christmas with Roger and his family. A few days later he was so weak that he had to enter the hospital. But though he was weak, Salva told those around him in the hospital what Jesus had done for him and that there was a home in heaven waiting for him.

Salva died on January 19, 1993. Though it was a time of great sadness for his family, the missionaries and all the others who loved him so much, for Salva there was joy, joy in seeing Jesus face-to-face–Jesus, the One who had given His life to pay for Salva's sins, the One whose power was great enough to set him free from heroin.

Teacher: Jose died before Salva. Salva's father died in 1986 or 1987.

www.ingramcontent.com/pod-product-compliance
Lightning Source LLC
Chambersburg PA
CBHW040749100426
42735CB00034B/119